The Spirit of
ALASKA

Text
Bill Harris

Photography
FPG
Gamma, Paris
Colour Library Books Ltd
International Stock Photography Ltd
Tim Thompson

Photo Editor
Annette Lerner

Design
Stonecastle Graphics

Commissioning
Andrew Preston

Editorial
David Gibbon
Mary Robertson

Production
Ruth Arthur
Sally Connolly
Karen Staff
Andrew Whitelaw

Director of Production
Gerald Hughes

CLB 2808
© 1992 Colour Library Books Ltd, Godalming, Surrey, England.
All rights reserved.
This 1992 edition published by Crescent Books,
distributed by Outlet Book Company, Inc., a Random House Company,
225 Park Avenue South, New York, New York 10003.
Printed and bound in Hong Kong.
ISBN 0 517 06592 4
8 7 6 5 4 3 2 1

The Spirit of
ALASKA

CRESCENT BOOKS
NEW YORK

St. Matthew Island

BERIN

BERING SEA

Attu Island

● Attu

Agattu Island   SEMICHI
          ISLANDS

NEAR
ISLANDS

Kiska Island   RAT
       ISLANDS

ALEUTIAN ISLANDS

      Amchitka Pass
     Gareloi I.
Amchitka Island   Tanaga   ANDREANOF ISLANDS
         Island
           Kagalaska I.
                                        Fort
                                       Glenn   Ak
Adak I.   ● Atka   Amukta I.   Umnak I. ●
                                              ● Nikolski
Amlia Island   Unalaska

ISLANDS OF THE FOUR
     MOUNTAINS

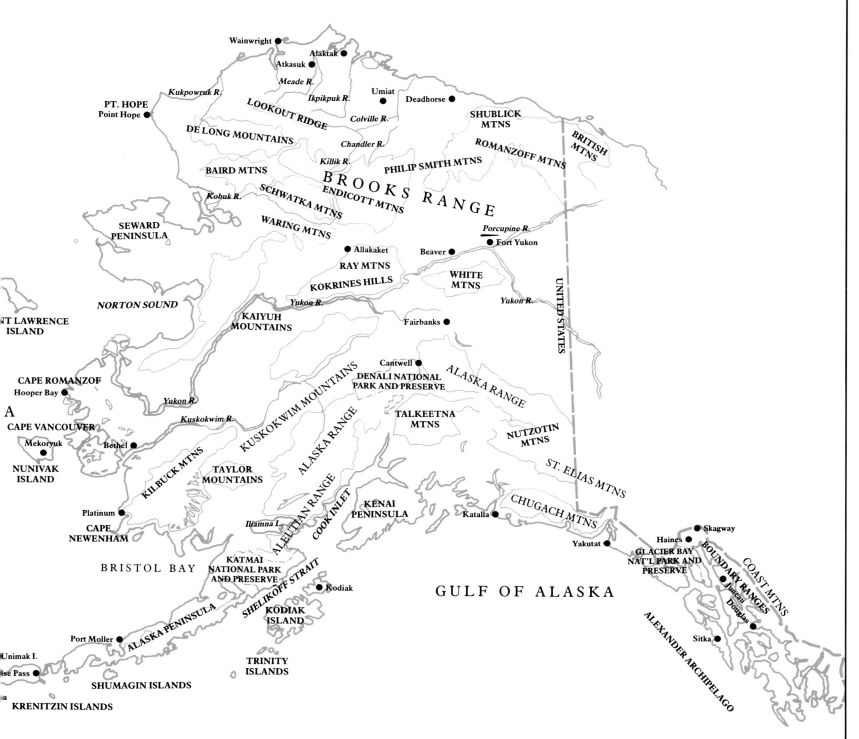

Wainwright
Alaktak
Atkasuk
Meade R.
Kukpowruk R.
Ikpikpuk R.
Umiat
Deadhorse
PT. HOPE
Point Hope
LOOKOUT RIDGE
Colville R.
SHUBLICK
MTNS
DE LONG MOUNTAINS
Chandler R.
ROMANZOFF MTNS
BRITISH
MTNS
BAIRD MTNS
Killik R.
PHILIP SMITH MTNS
B R O O K S   R A N G E
SCHWATKA MTNS
Kobuk R.
ENDICOTT MTNS
SEWARD
PENINSULA
WARING MTNS
Porcupine R.
Fort Yukon
UNITED STATES
Allakaket
Beaver
RAY MTNS
WHITE
MTNS
NORTON SOUND
KOKRINES HILLS
Yukon R.
Yukon R.
T LAWRENCE
ISLAND
KAIYUH
MOUNTAINS
Fairbanks
CAPE ROMANZOF
Hooper Bay
Cantwell
DENALI NATIONAL
PARK AND PRESERVE
ALASKA RANGE
A
KUSKOKWIM MOUNTAINS
CAPE VANCOUVER
Yukon R.
TALKEETNA
MTNS
NUTZOTIN
MTNS
Mekoryuk
Kuskokwim R.
ALASKA RANGE
Bethel
NUNIVAK
ISLAND
KILBUCK MTNS
TAYLOR
MOUNTAINS
ST. ELIAS MTNS
KENAI
PENINSULA
CHUGACH MTNS
Skagway
Platinum
ALEUTIAN RANGE
COOK INLET
Katalla
Haines
Yakutat
GLACIER BAY
NAT'L PARK AND
PRESERVE
BOUNDARY RANGES
COAST MTNS
CAPE
NEWENHAM
Iliamna L.
KATMAI
NATIONAL PARK
AND PRESERVE
SHELIKOFF STRAIT
GULF OF ALASKA
Juneau
Douglas
BRISTOL BAY
Kodiak
KODIAK
ISLAND
Sitka
Port Moller
ALASKA PENINSULA
ALEXANDER ARCHIPELAGO
Unimak I.
TRINITY
ISLANDS
se Pass
SHUMAGIN ISLANDS
a
KRENITZIN ISLANDS

PACIFIC OCEAN

The glory of the Inside Passage.

Back at the turn of the century, when most Americans would no sooner have planned a vacation in Alaska than contemplate a holiday in Siberia, an explorer predicted, quite accurately, that the day was not too far off when Alaska would be near the top of everyone's list of must-see places. But he added a warning: "If you are young, wait," he said. "It is not well to dull one's capacity for enjoyment by seeing the finest first."

But if he thought Alaska was too good to waste on the young, the message was lost on future Alaskans. The population today is among the youngest of the fifty states and most of them first arrived, if not as visitors, as workers or military personnel, with every intention of going home again before deciding that any other home would be dull by comparison. It's entirely appropriate. Alaska itself is one of the youngest places on earth. Its oldest rocks are about five-hundred million years old, compared to some five-billion years in other parts of the world, but many are relatively brand-new, having been spewed up in this century by forty-seven active volcanoes, or lifted to the surface by earthquakes and moved around by five-thousand glaciers whose work is still in progress.

Although the ancestors of America's Indians crossed a land bridge from Asia into Alaska more than fifteen thousand years ago, Alaska is quite young in terms of modern civilization, too. Nearly three million people were living in thirteen English colonies on the eastern edge of the continent before the first Europeans reached its northwestern corner.

The stories of the adventures of Christopher Columbus and others who explored the other side of North America are tame compared to the tale of the first voyages to Alaska. Seventeen years passed from the time that Tsar Peter the Great of Russia ordered the exploration, before word reached St. Petersburg that the mission was accomplished, and by then both the Tsar and Vitus Bering, the Danish mariner in charge of the expedition, were dead. Bering was not like the average explorer, but was an officer in the Russian Navy following orders he must have thought were bizarre. The assignment was to drag the materials to outfit and supply an ocean-going ship across six-thousand miles of Siberian wilderness, where there were no roads, no bridges and no relief from the world's most formidable climate. It took them two and a half years to make the trip, to build a ship and sail a few miles to St. Lawrence Island, at which point they turned back. They were at sea less than two months, and although they had proved that North America and Asia were separated by water, they never made it to Alaska. Even without a train of supplies, it took Bering another year and a half to march back to St. Petersburg, and when he got there he was treated as a failure.

But in spite of it, he was put in charge of an even more ambitious undertaking: to explore all of Siberia and then to sail down to Japan, and finally to map the west coast of North America from Mexico to whatever might happen to be at the northern end. He decided to start at the top, but eight years passed before the expedition set sail in the direction of America, with Bering in command of the square-rigger *Saint Peter*, followed by a smaller vessel, *Saint Paul*, commanded by Aleksei Chirikov. The ships were separated in the fog, and it was Chirikov's that sighted land first. He sent a longboat ashore but, even though the weather was fair, it disappeared. A few days later Chirikov sent another small boat to investigate and it, too, mysteriously vanished, leaving the *Saint Paul* without any way to land to collect any information about the place they had discovered. Bering himself, meanwhile, also spotted Alaska's St. Elias mountains and, considering his assignment fulfilled, he headed in the general direction of home. In spite of himself he was forced to put ashore on a small island by an outbreak of scurvy, and his men had no sooner landed when their ship slipped her anchor and was dashed to pieces on the rocks. During the winter more than half the crew, including Bering himself, died of scurvy and exposure to the cold, but in the spring the survivors went to work to build a new ship from the wreckage of the old one, and a few months later they were back in the relative safety of Siberia. As far as official Russia was concerned, the second Bering expedition was considered a bigger failure than the first, and all records of it were buried deep under the dust of government archives.

But there was an exception. Among the men who spent the winter on Bering Island was Georg Steller, a young German naturalist who found the place a treasure trove of wildlife. It was he who confirmed that the expedition had reached North America when he spotted a blue jay, a bird he had never seen except in pictures, which he knew existed only in the Western Hemisphere. But there were far more exotic creatures in the new land. Steller's book on the expedition was the first to introduce the rest of the world to fur seals, sea otters, sea cows and sea lions. He also described a huge species of cormorant and four new varieties of eider ducks, but it was the fur seals and sea otters that would send adventuresome Russian merchants in the direction of Alaska. The first of them was on his way before Steller organized his notes for the book, in fact. Impressed by the furs the survivors brought back, a Cossack sergeant named Emelian Basov decided to switch careers, and he talked thirty of his fellow soldiers into joining him on a voyage across a hundred miles of open ocean to track down some sea otters. The type of vessel they chose to make the trip should have doomed the enterprise right from the beginning. It was a flat-bottomed boat designed for travel on the Siberian rivers and, although it was rigged with sails, the design made it more practical to be propelled with poles or towed by oxen from a riverbank. But it could carry a lot of furs, and in four trips their little boat carried enough to earn nearly a million rubles, about six-million current American dollars, for the former soldiers, and this encouraged other adventurers to brave the Bering Sea in similar vessels. Eventually the sea otters began to shun the offshore islands, and the hunters were forced to range further in the direction of Alaska itself. Building bigger and more seaworthy ships, they were able to hopscotch along the 1,200-mile length of the Aleutian Islands, a process that took twenty years. In 1762, the year before the hunters finally reached Kodiak Island, a palace revolt in St. Petersburg placed Catherine II on the Russian throne and the future of Alaska took another turn.

The Russians had carefully guarded the secret of Alaska until then, but Catherine the Great had a sense of drama and she rocked the diplomatic community by casually announcing, in the midst of a glittering reception, that her people had established trading posts in the Aleutians and were ready to move on to the North American mainland itself. The European governments had taken note of Bering's discoveries, but they had also noted the Russian indifference to them, and the ambassadors could hardly contain themselves when Catherine smiled broadly and embellished her story by telling them that her explorers were, even as she spoke, planting metal plates engraved with her imperial symbol along America's West Coast. It was traditional for explorers to stick wooden crosses in the sand to claim territory, but the plaques had more permanence about them, and that was almost too much for the ambassadors to bear. Especially the Spanish ambassador. Within a year or two his government began financing a string of forts north of Mexico. If Catherine hadn't revealed her little secret, they might never have bothered. The French sent ships to have a look, too, and the English dispatched their master mariner, Captain James Cook, to map the northern Pacific and see to if he could figure out why the Russians were so interested in it. It never dawned on any of them that the fur trade might be worth so much effort. The Russians had all of Siberia, after all, and it abounded in sable which, as far as anyone knew, was the world's most valuable fur. Cook's men stumbled on the secret when the Indians gave them sea otter pelts, which they accidentally discovered were far more valuable to the Chinese than the finest sable. It started a race among British merchants to the Pacific Northwest, the Russians lost their sea otter monopoly and the days of the otter itself were severely curtailed. But in the meantime Catherine atoned for her sin of talking too much by allowing her subjects a free hand to trade in Alaskan furs with almost no government interference. It was a policy unheard-of in any country at the time, but especially in Russia, and hundreds of fortune-hunters descended on eastern Siberia with their eyes turned in the direction of Alaska.

But, though they had a foothold on the coast of North America, there was no Russian colony there worthy of the name until 1784, when an adventurer named Gregori Ivanovich Shelikhov arrived on the coast of Kodiak Island and began building the town he called Three Saints Bay. Once it was established, he petitioned Catherine to give him money to support it and to give him a monopoly on all the fur trade in Russian America. For several months he had every reason to believe she would, but without any explanation she suddenly turned him down. But she did give him an imperial sword, a gold medal and a portrait of herself.

She also let him keep his new town on Kodiak Island, and even though it was encumbered by several hundred thousand rubles of debt, he had a storehouse full of furs. And Shelikhov had the ear of one of Catherine's lovers, who managed to get him a limited monopoly on pelts taken within three hundred miles of his base. But in his enthusiasm, the young man went too far. In his original petition, Shelikhov had also asked for missionaries to Christianize the natives, for Siberian exiles to provide a labor force, and for the right to buy serfs to establish farms in Russian America. The twenty-three-year-old former soldier convinced the sixty-two-year-old Tsaritsa that she should grant all the requests and she did, with the notable exception of funds to finance them. The result was an increase in the population of Three Saints Bay by one-hundred-fifty souls, all of whom needed to be supported, a responsibility Catherine made quite clear would fall to the entrepreneur. They also needed to be transported to America, and that expense landed on Shelikhov's shoulders, too. He knew that if he refused to pay for their passage, to outfit the proposed missions and to feed the workers that there was a dungeon waiting in St. Petersburg with space for his name on the door.

Mercifully for him, Shelikhov died in 1795 just as word was reaching home that his colony wasn't what he had claimed it to be, and that the recently-arrived monks and farmers would probably starve to death. In the meantime, Catherine died, too, and power passed to her son, Paul, who had quite different views about Russian America. He didn't believe any of his subjects had any business leaving the country, but after a great deal of politicking, the merchants convinced him that other European powers who were beginning to discover democracy were likely to take over and allow the natives and their own subjects in the area to govern themselves. It was a terrible prospect for any Tsar, but especially for Paul, and he decided to let them go on colonizing North America to set up a buffer that would keep the idea of democracy from entering Russia through the back door.

The fur hunters got together and formed a consortium along the lines of the Hudson's Bay Company, which was moving westward across Canada into the Northwest, territory they considered theirs because Captain Cook had explored it. The Americans were moving in, too, and all the English-speaking trappers seemed to be doing their best to alienate the natives by breaking the tight Russian rule against selling them guns and whiskey. And if that competition wasn't stiff enough, the Russian merchants who had pooled their resources were still behaving like the rivals they had always been, and it soon became clear that their scheme was never going to work. The solution was completely at odds with Russian tradition. The Tsar uncharacteristically agreed to establish the Russian-American Company, a trading firm with power to maintain its own army and to conduct its own political affairs. The man in charge was Alexander Baranov.

The new governor had already been in Russian America for several years and knew the territory better than most. He eventually selected an almost-perfect spot to build a new seaport he called Archangel, which would later become known as Sitka. His intention was to make it the most important city in all the Russias, but the natives had other ideas and burned the fort to the ground, using guns supplied by traders out of New England to kill all the people inside. Baranov rebuilt it a short distance away at an even better site. He built other forts, too, ranging down the coast all the way to Fort Ross at the edge of Spanish California, but none of them had a chance, either. St. Petersburg refused to give them naval protection, and there were few Russians eager to make the long trip across Siberia to get to North America. Even at the height of the company's prosperity, the purely Russian population rarely went beyond about eight hundred. And prosperity was a sometimes thing because the Chinese, who were

Winter wonderland.

the best customers for sea otter pelts, frequently closed their doors to Western traders for long periods of time. The Americans and the British were aggressive competitors, too, and in spite of the monopoly the Tsar had given the Russian-American Company, Baranov's people were not exactly merchant princes. Finally, after the financial drain of the Crimean War, Russia was eager to throw in the towel, and in October 1867, a treaty went into effect making Alaska the property of the United States.

In light of recent history, it's hard to believe that Russia and the United States were ever as closely allied as they were in the 19th century. Russia was the only European power that provided help for the North in the Civil War, while all the others sided with the Confederacy; and when the Union was restored, Washington felt a debt of gratitude to the Tsar. Most of Russia's foreign trade was handled by American ships, which had special status in Russian ports except, ironically, in Alaska, where the American penchant for delivering guns and rum to the Indians had made them unwelcome. The 1849 gold rush in California was a boon to the Russian-American Company, which made almost as much money delivering picks and shovels to prospectors as shipping furs to China. And as much as the Russians loved Americans, they weren't too fond of the English. When it became apparent that British interests in Canada were in a position to take over Alaska, the proposition that there was no great love between the United States and the Mother country moved the Tsar's advisors to push for ceding the peninsula to Washington, to blunt the English threat of expanding its empire into Siberia. When gold was discovered in Western Canada in 1861, and thousands of Americans rushed in to claim it even though their country itself had no claim there, the Russians saw it as a golden opportunity, and their ambassador began canvassing influential American senators to find out what they'd be willing to pay for Alaska. The question became moot when Southern states began seceding from the Union, and by the time the Civil War was over, the Tsar seemed to have made up his mind to keep his North American colony after all. But William Seward, the American Secretary of State, had already made up his mind that he wanted the territory and offered $7.2 million for it. To everyone's surprise, the offer was accepted.

Seward negotiated the sale in complete secrecy, and when his proposal went to the Senate for approval the lawmakers were so full of resentment they nearly let the treaty die in Committee. When they finally did vote on it, they passed it by just a single vote. And they weren't finished yet. A month after the sale was approved, President Andrew Johnson sent a message to Congress asking them to come up with the money to pay for it. They referred the matter to the appropriations committee and then turned their attention to impeachment proceedings against the President. When Johnson was acquitted, his enemies began attacking the deal his Administration had made with Russia, and the debate over the appropriation, which didn't begin until the following June, was the most heated Washington had ever seen.

The American flag had been flying over Sitka for eight months by then, which helped make some of the rhetoric ridiculous, but they made their speeches anyway, and when the issue finally came to a vote the appropriation bill was passed by a huge margin. Tsar Alexander II finally got his $7.2 million, more than a year late, but Alaska itself came away from that summer with a tarnished image that still survives. Some Americans even today believe that it is a barren place unfit for human habitation, but nobody believes it wasn't one of the greatest bargains in American history, far better than Peter Minuit's purchase of Manhattan Island for twenty-four dollars.

But it would be a long, long time before Alaska became American territory in anything but name. According to the terms of the treaty, people living there, with the exception of "uncivilized native tribes," of course, would automatically have all the rights of American citizenship. They would also keep ownership of their land and their houses. And if they they decided they'd rather go back home to Russia, they had three years to make up their mind and the Americans would provide their transportation. But, like a lot of treaties, what's on paper doesn't always square with reality.

The Russians had been in North America for more than a hundred and twenty years by the time the sale was made, and Sitka itself was nearly sixty years old. They had established nearly fifty communities, and a high percentage of the families living in them had been in America for several generations. They had established schools, churches, parks, libraries, hospitals, a theater and even a college. The harbor at Sitka was one of the best-developed in North America and ships based there called at ports all over the world. It even had a lighthouse, one of the first on the West Coast. The city was far more sophisticated than San Francisco, and was well-known as the Paris of the Pacific. At the time the sale was negotiated, the Russian-American Company was beginning to expand from fur trading into mining and it had never been more prosperous. It seemed absurd that the Tsar would sell it all out from under them. But the terms of the deal seemed fair enough, and they were generally ready to make the best of a bad thing. As it turned out, it was worse than anyone could have predicted.

William Seward was a man in a hurry. He wanted take formal possession of the new territory right away and, knowing that Congress had other things on its mind, he arranged to have it placed under the control of the War Department as though it had been taken in battle. And what that meant was that Alaska would be occupied and governed by the military. Even though Seward had been a Senator himself and knew the ways of Congress, he was sure it wouldn't take more than a few weeks or months for them to set up a formal government with its own set of laws and a governor to enforce them.

But after the summer of 1868, when they talked about little else, Congress became silent on the subject of Alaska. Soon after they got around to paying for it they made it a special customs district to make sure that they could start collecting a return on their investment with duties on imports and exports. But it was not given the status of a territory as was traditional for all the other areas opened for settlement, and over the next seventeen years, eight different Congresses and four different Presidents pretended that Alaska didn't exist.

Like most other Americans at the time, the military authorities believed that Russian America had an Indian problem similar to the ones they themselves had faced in every other new territory they settled. The fact was that the Russians and the natives had gotten along remarkably well almost from the beginning, but the force of 250 men sent to claim Alaska, and their commanding general, Jefferson Davis, were all seasoned Indian fighters. Once the American flag was raised on October 18, 1867, they began a rampage of raping and looting and terrorizing the natives and Russians alike, all of whom began wondering about that clause in the treaty that gave them the rights and privileges of American citizens. Before long more soldiers arrived, and within a few months the newly-made American citizens began moving out, and within a few years the only Russian presence in Alaska was the Orthodox Church and its missionary priests.

But there were plenty of Americans to replace them. Hundreds arrived from California and the Northwest looking for new opportunities on the Last Frontier. It was a mixed bag of real estate operators, gamblers, businessmen, prostitutes and others, but they were all determined to make Alaska the last stop in their search for opportunity. But with no real government, no one in Alaska could buy or sell property. It wasn't possible to get married, or divorced, for that matter. Wills couldn't be enforced, and with no courts, laws couldn't be enforced, either, even though the citizens of Sitka had created their own government with rules everyone followed as best they could. Alaska had been touted as a land of endless bounty, but homesteaders couldn't mark out farms and independent trappers were forbidden to collect furs. The person in charge of the mess, General Davis, had problems of his own keeping peace among the peacekeepers, who had brought syphilis and drunkenness to the Indians and fear to the whites who never felt safe from them. He was visibly relieved when, after ten years of occupation, he and his troops were reassigned to Idaho to put the cantankerous Nez Perce Indians in their place.

The government in Washington wasn't completely insensitive to the problem, and not long after the purchase it gave some San Francisco entrepreneurs the exclusive right to exploit the fur resources of the Pribilof Islands. The idea, they said with perfectly straight faces, was to protect the coastline against poachers. Eventually the company expanded its interests to all of the Aleutians and part of the mainland. It was good business for them to promote law and order, and in the areas where they operated they did the government's job far better than the government itself. When the army was pulled out, the job of keeping the peace fell to the next highest American official, the collector of customs. But the job of governing such a huge territory without a code of laws wasn't exactly in his job description, which may explain why he went to Canada for urgent medical attention a few days after the responsibility was dumped on his shoulders. The hospital at Sitka had long since closed, along with the schools and other institutions, and the city had become a virtual ghost town during the years of the military rampage. Except for the areas controlled by the Alaska Commercial Company, complete anarchy had come to Alaska. In the wildest days of the Wild West, America had never experienced anything quite like it.

The government lurched forward to solve the problem, but once again its solution was almost ludicrous. The Treasury Department was put in charge because it already had people stationed in Alaska. Most of them were customs collectors, but some had experience in stopping the illegal flow of liquor, and if that wasn't exactly peacekeeping, it was as close as Washington felt it had to go. The Treasury agents followed the lead of Congress and the President and decided to do nothing at all. They probably felt quite justified because all of them were relatively new in their jobs and weren't too confident that their future in Alaska was very bright. Since establishing the Alaskan Customs District, Washington had neglected to pay its employees there, which naturally resulted in a rather high turnover. In his annual report for his first year in charge, the department's secretary made a strong recommendation to shut down the Alaska Customs District, in fact. The revenues they collected fell far short of the expense, if the expenses should ever happen to be paid, and the length of the coast and the Canadian border made it impossible for them to do the job anyway, he said. It was predictable that his request was ignored. It was said that in those days any mail received at the Treasury Department from anywhere in Alaska was usually thrown away unopened. Of course, that was some thirty-five years before citizens were required to mail in their income taxes.

The customs agents had petitioned the department for a warship to patrol the Alaskan waters to help ward off the very real threat of an Indian uprising, but, like every other plea from the North, it was lost in the shuffle. Finally, in desperation, they sent an SOS to a British task force stationed on Vancouver Island, and the Royal Navy responded by stationing one of its vessels in Sitka harbor for a month, until an American ship finally arrived. But the ship was just passing through. When its captain said that he had no orders to stay there, yet another petition was fired off to Washington, but this time it was sent to President Rutherford B. Hayes himself. The President responded by sending an even bigger ship, whose captain's orders were quite clear. His command was to include all of Alaska until Congress could get around to establishing a permanent government. A procession of vessels came and went after that, and for the next five years Alaska was governed from the bridge of a ship. And during those years, the command ship was virtually alone in Sitka harbor, which had once been one of the busiest in North America.

Finally, in 1884, Congress got its act together and passed a bill that gave Alaska its first governor and the set of laws that were in effect at the time in Oregon. It still wasn't perfect, but it was an improvement. And it was a clue to the attitude of the United States Congress that had debated, but not acted upon, more than twenty-five different proposals for Alaska's government, only to settle in the end for an idea to simply copy the laws of another state, which had little more in common with Alaska than that it was a long way from Washington. And at that, the congressmen casually added that the laws of Oregon would be in effect "so far as they are applicable." The bill gave Alaskans courts, but the judges weren't given a clue about what parts of the law applied. It gave them a law enforcement structure, but no funds for jails, or to transport lawbreakers from the scene of a crime to a court. It gave them guidelines for establishing county governments, but no means of creating the counties themselves. The governor was given the responsibility of reporting on conditions in the entire territory, but no funds or staff to move around it. In fact, although the new law specified salaries for officials, it didn't allow taxing of Alaskan citizens, and ordered that federal revenues collected there should not remain in Alaska, except to maintain the courts. The law, in its wisdom, stipulated that no one who wasn't a taxpayer could serve on a jury and, without taxation, Alaskans were denied the right of trial by jury. The act also failed to provide for a territorial legislature, or for a representative in Congress. And while it pretended to promote the establishment of schools, it appropriated just $25,000 for education, even though the population of the district at the time was estimated to be about thirty thousand. Governors grumbled, of course, but, like the Treasury men before them, they hardly had Washington's ear. In those days it took about three months to get a reply to a letter sent to the East Coast, assuming it was answered the same day it was received. But when more frequent steamship service began in the late '80s, the Postmaster General ruled it "inadvisable" to carry mail on every ship, and even when the shipowners offered to handle it free, the Post Office still refused to extend its service beyond one ship a month, and only the summer months at that.

Most Americans didn't really think too much about Alaska in those days, and the only pressure on official Washington came from the pitiful trickle of mail from the territory itself. The old myths still persisted that it was a worthless frozen wasteland, even though tourists began arriving in 1882, when passengers were carried on steamers and given short tours of the port cities while the freight was being unloaded. Many of them were also treated to cruises of Glacier Bay, one of the most incredibly beautiful bodies of water on the planet, but their numbers were limited, and except for the reports of scientific expeditions there was almost no way for average Americans to know what a treasure their government had bought for them, or to care that their representatives had turned their back on it. But apparently there were some who cared very much. In one of his annual reports, the governor charged that the Alaska Commercial Company, which had been given the monopoly on seal hunting, had lobbyists in Washington who routinely gave expert testimony to Congressional committees that Alaska was worthless and commissioned newspaper and magazine articles with the same message. They were also monopolizing the salmon fisheries, he claimed, and both industries were earning millions for outsiders, whose profits would be severely curtailed if they were subject to government controls. It goes without saying that a congressional committee held hearings into the matter and concluded that the company had not "used its political connections to obtain favors," although it didn't pretend that the company was without political connections. The same kind of lobbying had also apparently resulted in a complicated law that prevented Alaskans from cutting trees on public land which, according to the same law, was nearly all of Alaska. Average citizens were restricted to townsites, and only corporations were allowed to claim land beyond their borders. The result was that any timber used for building, or even for containers to ship produce out of the territory, had to be imported from Oregon or Washington.

It was not surprising that in its first quarter-century as an American possession, Alaska's population hardly changed, although it wasn't easy to tell. The district was excluded from the 1870 census, and when the national population was counted ten years later, only one census-taker was hired to cover all of Alaska. By 1890, the official estimate was that there were slightly more than 32,000 Alaskans. But ten years after that the number was almost exactly doubled, and Alaska seemed to have a future at last.

The reason was as old as the story of America itself: there was gold up there.

Back in 1880, Joe Juneau and Richard Harris went prospecting for gold near Gastineau Channel, and when they found it other prospectors flocked in and together they formed a special mining district, at first known as Harrisburg, but later as Juneau. It was the first new town in American Alaska, made possible by a quirk in the already quirky law that allowed miners to organize and govern themselves. Ordinarily, such communities were temporary, but in addition to the placer gold Harris and Juneau had discovered, others found hard-rock deposits and gold digging flourished there for more than fifty years. But although the town's population grew to 1,200 in its first decade, it was hardly a classic gold rush. That was a few years off in the future.

Most of the fortune hunters who converged on Juneau eventually wandered off to the north in the direction of the Yukon looking for easier pickings. Among them was George Carmack, whose wanderings took him across the border into Canada's Yukon Territory, where his Indian brothers-in-law, Skookum Jim and Tagish Charlie, led him to Rabbit Creek, near the Klondike River, where they picked up a fist-sized gold nugget. The three men staked their claims, and even before they were registered, hundreds of sourdoughs were driving stakes into the banks of every creek in the area, and every one of them was flowing with gold. It was almost a year later that the miners began arriving in San Francisco with suitcases full of

Teamwork on Knik Lake.

gold dust, and people as far away as New York then began packing their own suitcases for a trip to the Klondike. Almost none of nearly a hundred thousand people who headed in the general direction of Alaska knew that the Klondike was in Canada, but it didn't really matter. The best way to get there was through Skagway, and less than half the fortune hunters who made it that far managed the trip across the mountains to Dawson and the Klondike gold fields. Many of them went home again, but hundreds stayed, and over the next dozen years they seemed to find gold everywhere they looked. Just as important, they also discovered other minerals, including coal and iron. Most important of all, the American public had finally discovered Alaska, and their representatives in Washington found that they couldn't go on ignoring it.

Congress got rather busy with Alaskan issues, in fact. It began by extending the Homestead Act to allow settlers to take title to public land. The amount of land a family could claim was only half the acreage customary in other parts of the country, but it was better than nothing. Congress also gave railroads the right to expand into Alaska, and it provided a new criminal code. It gave the settlers the right to incorporate their own communities and to tax themselves to support them. In less than three years, some fifty new federal laws were promulgated for the benefit of Alaska. Among them was a touching attempt to save Yukon prospectors from starvation, which moved the conferees to appropriate $200,000. Apparently moved by lifelong visions of Santa Claus, and vaguely remembering that the North Pole was up there somewhere near Alaska, they also approved funds to have reindeer imported from Norway to carry the supplies across the mountains. Most of the reindeer starved to death, but few of the prospectors did. Most of the destitute miners were in Canada and the Ottawa government had taken care of them. But after the flurry of activity, Alaska was still without a legislature, which it didn't get until 1912, six years after it sent its first voteless delegate to Congress. In the same year, Washington formally decreed that "the Constitution shall have the same force and effect within Alaska as elsewhere in the United States." Forty-five years had passed since a treaty had guaranteed Alaskans "all the rights, advantages and immunities of citizens of the United States." In those years, the federal government had lavished $35 million on the development of Alaska and had earned $450 million from its resources.

With control over its own affairs, Alaska seemed to be on its way toward a bright future, but old habits die hard and officials in Washington still seemed determined to keep the territory on ice. (Even today, Washington classifies all of Alaska except Anchorage as rural, even rejecting Juneau, the capital city, as anything resembling an urban center.) The new legislature had been designed to be toothless, but it managed to get things done. Population figures were growing by leaps and bounds when railroads made it easier to get there, and little by little Alaska began to seem less a colony of some great imperial power and more a working partner in a going concern. Then, in 1940, everything began to change for the better. Preparations for war brought airports, which in turn brought airline links to the lower forty-eight states. New highways were built and military bases opened, and by the time the war was over in 1945 Americans had begun to look at Alaska through new eyes. More and more of them decided it was just what they were looking for as a place to live, and although the legislation of 1912 had guaranteed them all the rights granted by the Constitution, they longed for statehood. The first attempt to have the issue debated in Congress was introduced in 1916, and there were dozens of similar statehood bills introduced after that. But through it all, Congress seemed to still be up to its old tricks. As recently as 1954, when the Senate approved statehood, but the house refused to vote on it, it was argued in the capitol that the climate in Alaska was so hostile that "brief exposure means instant death." Fortunately, cooler heads prevailed and finally, on January 3, 1959, President Dwight D. Eisenhower formally welcomed Alaska as the forty-ninth state. Significantly, the crowds that celebrated congressional approval the previous June danced under the midnight sun in shirtsleeves.

One of the most incredible things about Washington's long-standing determination to pretend that Alaska doesn't exist is that it is so hard to ignore. The statistics are staggering. With more than 570,000 square miles, it is twice as big as Texas with 36,000 square miles to spare. Juneau, its capital city, covers a thousand more square miles of territory than the entire state of Delaware, making it the largest city in the United States by area, although almost as many people live in Ft. Wayne, Indiana. The nearly 2,400-mile trip from east to west crosses four time zones, and is roughly equal to the distance between New York and Los Angeles. From north to south, Alaska extends nearly 1,400 miles, about the same distance a flier logs on a trip from Chicago to Phoenix. Its nearly 44,000 miles of seacoast, bordering two oceans and three seas, is fifty percent longer than all of the continental United States combined. It has three million lakes, twelve major rivers, 119 million acres of forests and the highest mountain in North America, not to mention seventeen of the top thirty peaks on the continent. But to most Americans, the most surprising statistic of all is that there are fewer automobiles registered in Alaska than in the sixty-eight-square-mile District of Columbia. It's true that there are about a hundred thousand more people in the Capital, but more important, the roads are better. There are only a few thousand miles of paved roads in all of Alaska, and many of them aren't connected with one another, which naturally leads to yet another statistic: more people in Alaska have private pilot certificates than in any other state.

Compared to other states, Alaska is still very much the wild frontier. In spite of impressive population increases in recent years, there is still less than one Alaskan for every square mile of territory, a figure that could be misleading considering that more than sixty-three percent of them live in cities like Anchorage, where the density shoots up to about one hundred per square mile. The total number of Alaskans, in the neighborhood of 525,000, is only slightly higher than the population of Denver, Colorado.

Even Denverites are awed by the mountains in Alaska, and Americans who a few years ago considered the Rockies to be the best wilderness experience their country had to offer are finding something even better in the forty-ninth state. But Alaska is something more than a wilderness experience. People who move there, whether they're oilfield workers from Texas and Oklahoma, New Yorkers fed up with crowds, or transplanted Maine fishermen, are quite pleased to be identified as Alaskans even though their accents give them away. About half the people who live there now lived in another part of the country just a few years ago, and when they moved north much more changed about them than their address. Alaska isn't the sort of place where you simply make your home, it's a place you get involved in; a place you think about and talk about all the time. It's a prime topic of conversation along Fourth Avenue in Anchorage and on Front Street in Nome. Local newspapers in every town refer to the rest of the world, including Alaska's forty-nine sister states, as "Outside," and it's their style to use a capital "O" when they write it. But they don't report much from out there unless it has something to do with the quality of life up here. And why not? The government ignored them for nearly half a century, and Washington often still seems to have a problem identifying with them. The experience gave Alaskans the same kind of independent spirit that infected the citizens of New England back in the 1700s. Boston, after all, is just about the same distance from London as Juneau is from Washington.

Even in a world where jumbo jets have reduced that distance to a matter of hours, and hundreds make the trip every day, there are still plenty of people who believe that Alaska is a land of permanent ice and snow. And even though there is evidence that the congressman who said even short exposure to the climate could result in instant death was wrong, it isn't hard to find people who still accept it as fact. Sure, it gets cold in Fairbanks, as cold as sixty below zero at times, but in the summer it is just as common for the temperature to reach the mid-eighties there. And Barrow, the northernmost town in the state, is a good bit warmer than Fairbanks year round, even though it isn't far from the Arctic icepack. And in more than a third of the state, the sun shines for twenty-four hours a day for as long as eight weeks in summer. In the Southeastern Panhandle, it's a rare winter day when the mercury dips to zero. And more than once, the route of the annual Iditarod sled dog race had to be altered because there was no snow at the traditional starting point in Anchorage.

But almost nobody goes to Alaska to enjoy the climate. These days, the most popular tourist excursions are made aboard cruise ships from Vancouver and San Francisco that go up the inside passage among the islands and peninsulas of the Panhandle. As the crow flies, the southeast corner of the state is only four-hundred miles long, not far by Alaskan standards, but the boat trip from Ketchikan to Skagway is more than twice as long, and by anybody's standards it is easily the most spectacular voyage in the world, especially on ships that include

Glacier Bay in their itinerary. The view from the deckchair includes misty islands and craggy mountains, rugged fjords and sparkling glaciers, plus all the comforts of home and then some. But for Alaskans themselves, there is a better way to enjoy the Panhandle. They use public transportation. In an area whose dozen communities aren't connected by roads, people get from one to another on state-run ferries, the larger of which make weekly runs from Seattle and, for half the cost, from Prince Rupert in British Columbia. Smaller ones serve places with names like Angoon and Hoonah. The best part is that ferry passengers can get off at any stop, stay as long as they like and continue the trip without any extra charge. There's no extra charge for luggage, either, and in Alaska carry-on gear usually includes a kayak, a canoe or a bicycle. The ferries aren't quite as luxurious as the cruise ships, but they are surprisingly comfortable, and they operate all year round. Better still, people who take their cars aboard the larger vessels during the winter months pay for the vehicle but not for themselves, and service within the state is free for senior citizens between October and May.

The ferries and the cruise ships serve just a corner of Alaska, only about a dozen miles wide at some points, but for most it's a corner of paradise. On the inland side, the Coast Mountains rise up as high as twenty thousand feet above sea level, and unlike most of the world's mountains, they begin at sea level. And dotted among them are mile after mile of glaciers punctuated by flower-strewn alpine meadows. The thousands of islands in the waterway itself are covered with lush forests of spruce and hemlock teeming with wildlife, including grizzly bears and bald eagles. And although the Panhandle is a land of ruggedly beautiful wilderness, it is also where most Alaskans live, and where the story of human life on the Last Frontier is still very much alive.

For most visitors, the story begins at Ketchikan, perched on the side of a three-thousand-foot mountain and extending on pilings out over the water. Appropriately, the self-styled "Gateway to Alaska" is rich with the heritage of the Tlingit Indians, who were the first to discover that the waters there were alive with salmon, and the town has the largest collection of totems in the world. It is also a good spot to begin a trip into the wilderness, as is Wrangel, a busy lumber port about eighty miles to the north. At the edge of Mitkov Island, a bit further north, the fishing port of Petersburg is a carefully-preserved reminder of the Norwegian fishermen who arrived there in the 1890s, just as the Russian heritage still lives in nearby Sitka.

The most "American" stop on the trip up the Inside Passage is Juneau, a modern city complete with sprawling suburbs and fast-food restaurants, but a leisurely stroll along a downtown street leads across meadows and through thick forests to the top of a four-thousand-foot mountain; a choice of two, in fact. Across the way is Admiralty Island, all by itself worth a trip from anywhere. Its million acres are completely untouched by the hand of man. It has snowfields and glaciers, hundreds of lakes and spectacular waterfalls. It is covered with a thick rainforest that shelter an incredible number of deer and brown bears, and its seven-hundred-mile shoreline is a paradise for sealions and whales. It also, according to some estimates, has the largest population of bald eagles in the world.

Glacier Bay, a short trip northwest of Juneau, is where the Inside Passage experience reaches its climax. When the early explorers and trappers opened the Alaska Panhandle for civilization, the bay didn't exist. Formation began in the 1750s, and in the years since then melting ice has created a body of water nearly sixty-five miles long, and the work is still in progress. Some twenty major glaciers form great cliffs of ice as much as two hundred feet high along the shore and, as the water undermines them, huge chunks break away and crash with a roar into the bay as massive icebergs.

Cruise ships generally head south again after treating their passengers to Glacier Bay, but the whole interior of Alaska is up there to the north, and visitors whose appetites have been whetted for more get there though the same gateways the sourdoughs used back in the gold rush days – the towns of Haines and Skagway. Neither of them has changed much since the 1890s, except they are much less crowded, and to many Alaskans it's what makes them a perfect place to live.

It's possible to drive or take a bus from Skagway to the Alaska Highway and into the interior all the way to Fairbanks. But a much simpler route into the Alaskan interior is through Anchorage, a city that usually surprises first-time visitors with its very un-Alaskan skyscrapers,

Downtown Anchorage.

four-lane highways and its international airport. But for all that, Anchorage has a setting that couldn't be duplicated anywhere but in Alaska. Off to the east, the peaks of the Chugach Mountains are reminder enough of the rugged frontier, but in the west and south the Aleutian Range, with its volcanic peaks rising as many as twelve thousand feet right from sea level, are even more dramatic. And, off to the north, the view of the Alaska Range includes the awesome Mount McKinley. Northeast of the city, the Matanuska Valley is fertile farmland that produces incredibly large vegetables, thanks to the long hours of summer sunlight; and a short trip to the southeast leads to the spectacular Prince William Sound, a compact version of the terrain of the Panhandle, with fjords and forested islands, dense rainforest and exotic wildlife.

The Sound became infamous in 1989 with a massive oil spill, and although it has since recovered it has become a symbol of what many Alaskans consider the beginning of the end for their paradise on earth. Others say that without oil Alaska would still be the stepchild of the fifty states. But whatever side they're on, no one in Alaska denies that nothing in their history compares to the discovery of the oilfield at Prudhoe Bay.

U.S. Navy explorers discovered oil deposits on Alaska's North Slope as far back as 1886, and wildcatters found more over the years. But it wasn't until 1968 that a commercially-feasible strike was made by the Atlantic-Richfield Company. It very nearly didn't happen. ARCO had spent nearly half a million dollars on a dry hole in the North Slope, and very nearly packed it in before giving it one more try in Prudhoe Bay. The well produced 1,152 barrels a day, but company officials cautiously characterized it as a "very rank wildcat." Geologists disagreed, and before long the oil rush was on. Boosters were thrilled at the prospect of unprecedented growth, but environmentalists weren't so sure. While the former were predicting that the find would put Alaska into the same category as the Middle East, the latter were asking how they intended to get the stuff to market.

The first answer was to build a highway from the Fairbanks area north to the Arctic. But the road was a disaster. It was bulldozed out of the tundra, creating a kind of trench that filled with windblown snow in the winter and became a shallow, water-filled canal in the spring and summer. But, confident that there was an answer out there somewhere, the big oil companies eagerly bid on North Slope leases, and in a single day the State of Alaska earned more than $900 million.

Meanwhile, the oil companies decided that the best way to get the crude out of Alaska was through an eight-hundred-mile pipeline from the North Slope to Valdez on Prince William Sound. Engineering and environmental problems held up the project for almost five years, but construction began in midsummer 1974, and oil began flowing through it three years later. Money was no object, and Fairbanks boomed with workers and engineers whose combined income added some $800,000 a day to the city's economy. Oil is still bringing jobs to Alaska as well as new people and more money. The state was earning about $300 million a year from its natural resources before the pipeline was finished, and when the oil reached Valdez the figure jumped to $1 billion.

The money translates to better roads, schools and hospitals and other social services, with lower taxes in the bargain. But the jury is still out on the question of whether the oil boom may destroy the unique Alaskan lifestyle, and the spill in Prince William Sound scored a sorry victory for the people who think it will. There is no joy in saying "I told you so," when you're knee deep in slippery crude oil trying to save an otter from hyperventilation. And people on both sides of the argument know that, as sure as God made those wonderful mountains, there is a lot more oil under Alaska's North Slope than the Trans-Alaska Pipeline can ever handle. A conservative estimate says that the amount of oil and gas yet undiscovered there is probably equal to more than a third of all the oil and gas in all of North America, including what's already being exploited in Alaska.

The jobs the boom has created has lured thousands to Alaska, but just as many thousands have been drawn there by the peace of the wilderness, the clear expanse of the skies, the majesty of the mountains. And while people still living Outside debate world affairs, the debate among Alaskans centers around what is becoming of their own world. Roads cut through the tundra and the sound of motorboats destroys the peace of quiet river valleys. But if the danger of the intrusion of civilization in such a vast country, where there are hundreds of square miles no man has ever seen, may seem ludicrous to someone from the Northeast, the danger is very real in the eyes of a great many Alaskans. From their point of view, they may be right. But even the most dedicated nature-lovers among them are part of the problem.

Alaskans may not have as many cars as their fellow Americans, but they depend on them just as much. They enjoy snowmobiles, too, and though they don't want to see a gas station every few miles, they do expect to be able to find one before their tank is empty. They need stores to provide them with food and clothing and they, like the gas stations, have to be supplied by truck, which creates a need for better roads and adds a bit more pollution to the environment. And so it goes. Everyone who tries to escape from civilization unwittingly takes a little civilization along with them.

Even the native Americans in Alaska have been touched by civilization. They hunt with rifles, fish from plywood boats, and catch salmon in nets made of nylon. They still use fishhooks crafted from animal bones, but more often have machine-made metal hooks at the end of their lines. They catch birds with steel wire snares rather than the willow their ancestors used, and when they turn them into a meal the side dishes are likely to come from a can. They still make their coats from caribou hides, but under them are blue jeans and shirts made by machine. And their villages are often marked with signs warning outsiders that they are private property, a concept far removed from their tradition.

But at least in the forseeable future, civilization is fighting a losing battle in Alaska. The people there are still huddled together in cities and towns, and some tourists have seen more of the state than many Alaskans themselves. Ask one of them about a lake or a valley or a mountain pass and they'll probably say that they've flown over it dozens of times, but have never been on the ground there. The place is almost too big to comprehend, and the people who know it best are the bush pilots, most of whom haven't experienced it close-up or felt much of it underfoot.

A lot of different people are given credit for blazing the trails in the air over Alaska, but the idea that planes couldn't function in the climate was put to rest by General Billy Mitchell, who flew from New York City to None in 1920. Four years later, a former Army pilot, Ben Eilson, flew the mail from McGrath to Fairbanks in three hours, a service that usually took more than two weeks by dogsled, and legend says that with his flight the future of Alaska was changed. But Ben's own future as a mail pilot wasn't very secure. When he crashed during a landing at the Fairbanks ballpark, the Post Office decided to go back to dogsleds. Ben flew off in the other direction to convince the officials in person that they were making the wrong decision, and while he was in the Washington area he developed a new type of ski gear for large airplanes. The government wasn't interested in either Eilson or his invention, and he went back home to join an air exploration of the Arctic Ocean, which included the first flight over the North Pole, with George H. Wilkins, from Point Barrow to Spitsbergen in Norway. The flight made him a national hero and got him a new job as manager of a new Alaskan Airline. He lost his life in 1929 on a mission to save the crew of an icebound ship off the coast of Siberia, but he was followed by hundreds of others who even now routinely land their planes on glaciers, and provide the only link between isolated villages and the outside world. And in a land with more exotic wildlife than East Africa, they have added Beavers and Widgeons, Otters and Piper Cubs to the list.

As is the case everywhere else in Alaska, conversations with bush pilots usually revolve around what the future holds in store. With more territory than any other state protected in National Parks and National Forests, it is likely to be forever wild. But the future of its economy may not be set in stone. At the moment, oil is at the center of it, and there is enough black gold in Alaska to keep the world's engines running for a long time to come. But in an increasingly energy-conscious world, who can say how long it might be needed? Fortunately, it isn't Alaska's only resource, but there might be a lesson to be found in one of its first enterprises as an American territory.

When William Seward bought the place, his ambassador in Russia assured him it was worth at least "fifty millions of dollars" considering its ports, its mines and its furs. But the profit motive often goads men into looking beyond the obvious. Some enterprising businessmen were sipping cocktails one night in San Francisco when one of them asked, "What does Alaska have that we don't?" They all looked into their glasses for an answer and, lo and behold, there it was right under their noses; or rather it wasn't. The answer was ice. In those days, ice was shipped to California around Cape Horn from New England. The cost of getting it there made icewater and on-the-rocks cocktails a luxury only the super-rich could afford. And, these men figured, you could get very rich in the ice business if you kept your expenses down.

They established themselves at Sitka, where there was a pond big enough to satisfy all the ice requirements of the whole state of California, and began cutting big blocks that could fetch seventy-five dollars a ton back home. But they hadn't done their homework. The temperature can go down as low as twenty below zero along the edge of the Panhandle, but it gets above the freezing mark for long periods, too and, in fact, the average temperature around Sitka is higher than in New England, where the competition was. By the end of the second winter, the icemen concluded that the only way to keep their business alive was to move inland where it was colder. But it wasn't a total loss, the ice was insulated in sawdust for shipping, which made it necessary for them to build a sawmill near their pond, and by the time refrigeration made their original business obsolete, they had a profitable lumber business to fall back on.

Alaskan husky.

A river of ice from the Harding Icefield slinks down to meet the sea.

Facing page: Ruth Glacier on Mount McKinley.

Reflections in a quiet land – the Harding Icefield.

Fragile tundra – a harsh environment.

A bleak, beautiful river in Denali National Park.

Mineral Creek near Valdez on Prince William Sound.

Facing page: the busy
village of Homer at the
end of the Sterling
Highway.

Alaskaland, a
recreation of old
Fairbanks.

Above: old and new in
the city of Juneau.

Juneau's houses often
cling to steep hillsides.

Facing page: a bit of
old New England in
Juneau.

Snug and cozy, woodland cabins in Valdez.

Winter morning icicles glisten in McGrath, a town on the Kuskokwim River.

Moonlit and snowbound – an empty house in McGrath.

A bird's view of the Alaska Range.

Right: the welcome mat is out on a winter's night in McGrath.

A Nome streetscape. Nome is the transportation hub of the state.

The morning sun has no effect on the winter snows of McGrath.

A derelict house in the ghost town of Iditarod.

A well-deserved break at Anvik, western Alaska.

Loving care on the Iditarod trail.

Facing page: Iditarod champion Libby Riddles and friend.

In for repairs – a husky team takes a lot of looking after.

Removing painful snowballs – huskies are made to wear snow socks to avoid this.

A veterinarian team makes a house call during the Iditarod Race.

Left: an Iditarod sled dog sometimes gets too tired to eat.

Airlifting out for those race dogs just too weary to carry on.

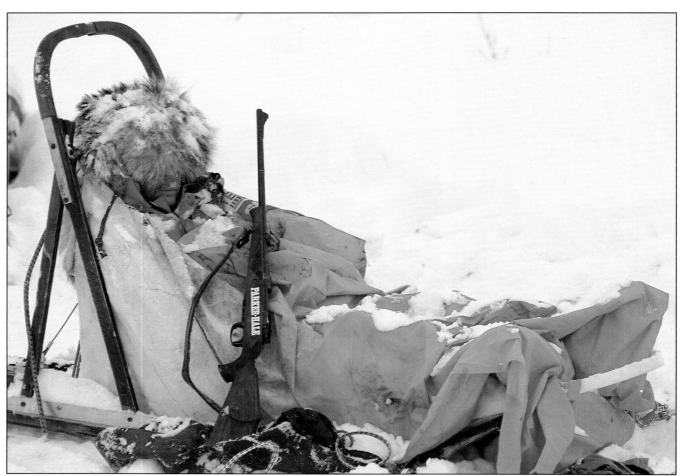

Mushers are usually as tired as their huskies during the marathon Iditarod Race.

A sled is a great bed, if you're exhausted.

With a snowmobile up front, is it still called a dogsled? Kotzebue in winter.

Picnic lunch – Iditarod entrant Clair Philip prepares dog food on the trail.

Hawaiian Kevin Saike has a rest stop during the gruelling Iditarod.

Mountain kingdom,
Denali National Park.

Scientists at work on
the Juneau Icefield.

Explorer Glacier in the Portage Glacier Recreation Area.

The Delta River reflecting the peaks of the Alaska Range.

*Above the treeline in
Denali National Park.*

*Above: the Portage
River flows through
Kenai Fjords National
Park.*

*Glacier Bay Park
covers some three
million acres.*

*The Portage River,
which rises in Chugach
National Forest.*

The sharp peak of Mount Kimball rises to over 10,000 feet.

A glacier cuts a path on the face of Mount McKinley.

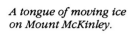

A tongue of moving ice on Mount McKinley.

Mount McKinley's southeastern face.

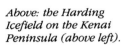

Above: the Harding Icefield on the Kenai Peninsula (above left).

Aialik Bay near Caines Head Recreation Area.

The Chugach Mountains in southern Alaska.

*A glacier of the
Harding Icefield meets
Aialik Bay.*

Mount McKinley, almost 18,000 feet high.

Mount McKinley's glacier-carved slopes.

Left: a glacier-fed bay, Kenai Peninsula.

A "river" of eternal ice that creeps instead of flows.

Mount McKinley (right) is also called Denali, which means "The Great One."

Ruth Glacier, Mount McKinley.

Mount McKinley is North America's highest peak.

Mendenhall Glacier, which is over ten miles long, near Juneau.

Harding Icefield, Ailalik Bay.

Right: Adams Inlet, Glacier Bay.

An ice wall in Muir Inlet, Glacier Bay.

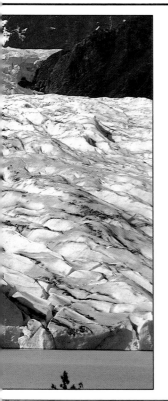

Right: a tidewater glacier on the Kenai Peninsula.

The Last Frontier –
western Alaska.

Right: Mount Drum
and Gulkana Airport.

Bush pilots' skiplanes
on Iditarod Lake.

Right: a lifeline to the world outside.

Right: a float plane on Anchorage's Lake Hood.

Left: Anchorage Lake, the world's biggest floatplane base.

The Anchorage fleet is a boon for sightseers.

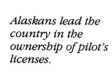

Alaskans lead the country in the ownership of pilot's licenses.

*Left: Anchorage
International Airport.*

*Below: Anchorage's
helicopter fleet.*

A squadron of floatplanes.

All dressed up for the Anvik winter.

Facing page: faces from Kotzebue.

Below: an Inuit woman.

All set for nighttime sled driving.

Fred Andree, musher.

Memories of goldrush days.

Libby Riddles, musher.

Joe Redington, a founder of the Iditarod Race.

"The beard on his chin was as white as the snow." Clement C. Moore.

A descendant of the Vikings.

A descendant of the original Alaskans.

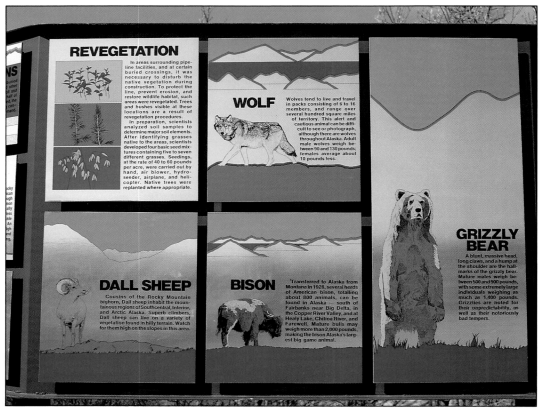

An information sign identifies wildlife.

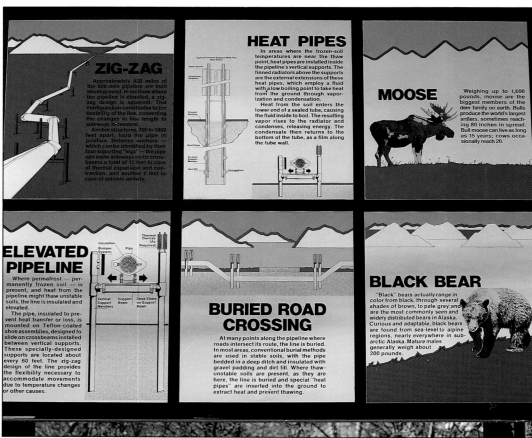

The anatomy of the Trans Alaska Oil Pipeline.

A reminder of the Russian presence in Juneau.

Alaska Department of Fish and Game

Each year from April to August the Delta bison herd is often visible from this spot. During the summer months the herd forages along the Delta river floodplain, moving to the Delta area in winter. At the closest they are two miles distant, binoculars or spotting scopes are helpful. Alaska's present day bison herds originated from a 1928 transplant from Montana and have thrived in this area and a few other areas around the state. The herd is kept in balance with its range through controlled hunting as bison rarely experience predation.

A guide to the Delta Junction bison herd.

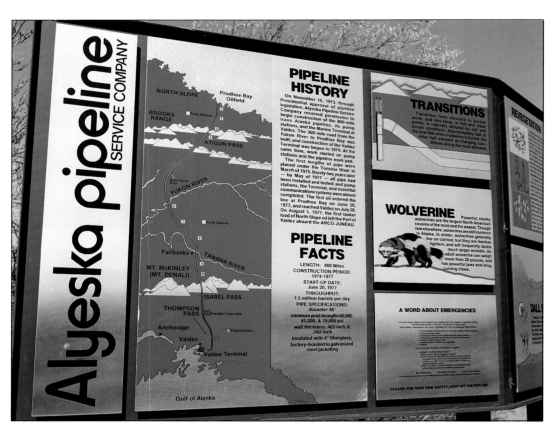

The story of the pipeline.

The 800-mile pipeline crosses rugged country.

Oil began flowing through the pipeline toward Valdez in 1977.

Raising the pipeline prevents thaw at ground level.

Mendenhall Glacier is north of Juneau.

A memorial at Isabel Pass for the Road Commission's first president.

A Denali National Park homesteader.

The Toklat grizzly bear is a native Alaskan.

Grizzlies thrive in Denali National Park.

Grizzly bears are among the world's most dangerous creatures.

*Black bears abound in
the southeast of the
state.*

*Bears are best avoided,
but hard to resist.*

Kittiwakes nesting on Pribilof cliffs.

Below: fur seal beachmasters and their harems.

Bison in search of a green meal.

Below: a bear waits for a meal to come to him.

A caribou leaps for safety.

Right: both male and female caribou have antlers.

The caribou's color blends into the brush.

Above and right: seals and birds share a superb view in Glacier Bay National Park.

Left: seals are one of the star attractions of Glacier Bay.

*The heart of Glacier
Bay National Park.*

*Migrating caribou on
the Kobuk River.*

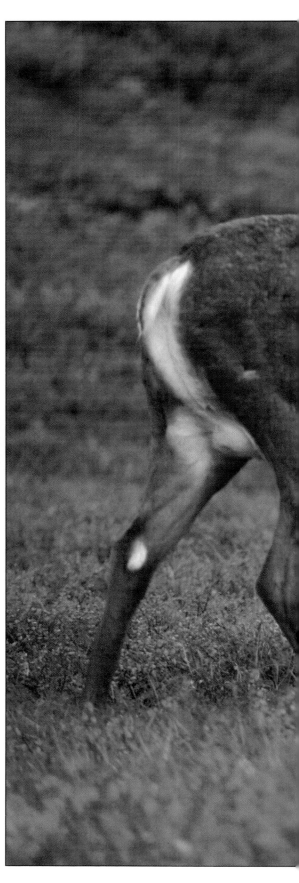

*A bull caribou in his
fall finery.*

This page: they're off! The Iditerod begins in Anchorage.

The last leg of the Iditarod is over the Bering Sea.

Below: the Iditarod trail leads from Anchorage to Nome. Teamwork gets them there.

A rest stop on Eagle Island during the Iditarod Race.

Above: an Anchorage traffic jam.

Leaving civilization behind at the beginning of the Iditarod.

*Not every musher will
see the Iditarod finish
line.*

*All of Nome gathers to
cheer the winners of
one of the hardest
races in the world.*

Facing page: the George Parks Highway passes Mount McKinley.

Right: Shaktoolik on Norton Sound.

The Governor's Mansion in the Alaskan state capital, Juneau.

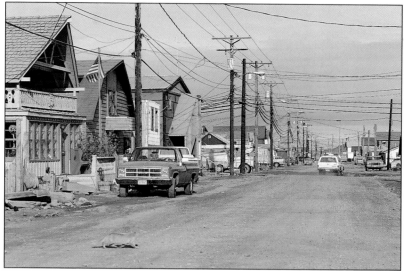

*Above: downtown
Nome in western
Alaska.*

*Above: a Nome
streetscape.*

*Fourth Avenue,
Anchorage.*

*Facing page: the
crossroads of the world,
Anchorage.*

*Anchorage's
convention center.*

Well built against the wind and snow – an Alaskan trapper's cabin.

A roadside rest at Ester, west of Fairbanks.

Snowmobiles are a great boon for Alaskan living.

Below: alternative transportation.

The Inuit village of Kotzebue, north of the Arctic Circle.

Kotzebue lies close to a major zinc mine, which provides many jobs for the Inuit.

Kotzebue is a place where traditional and modern lifestyles blend.

Youngsters get in touch with their heritage in Nome.

In learning traditonal dances, Nome school children follow in the footsteps of their ancestors.

Jumping for joy in Nome – the blanket toss is very popular.

The art of self defense as practiced in Nome.

Native dancers – in western Alaska you often have to make your own fun.

Joyful traditions are still celebrated by the Inuit people.

Inuit children perform traditional movements.

An Inuit performance in Kotzebue.

*Dipnetting in the
Twentymile River near
Fairbanks.*

*Above: panning for
gold, which it is still
possible to find near
Fairbanks.*

Gold-seekers. The Alaskan Interior was opened up by gold miners.

Turnagain Arm near the town of Portage.

Right: the Nenana River, a glacier-fed river in the Alaska Range.

Facing page: thaw in Denali National Park.

The Delta River, born in the Alaska Range.

The snowy slopes of Mount Juneau.

Winter settles on the marina at Valdez.

Steamboating on the Tanana River near Fairbanks.

A luxury cruise liner calls at Juneau harbor.

Cruising through the ice floes in Glacier Bay.

Above: a safe haven in Seward yacht harbor.

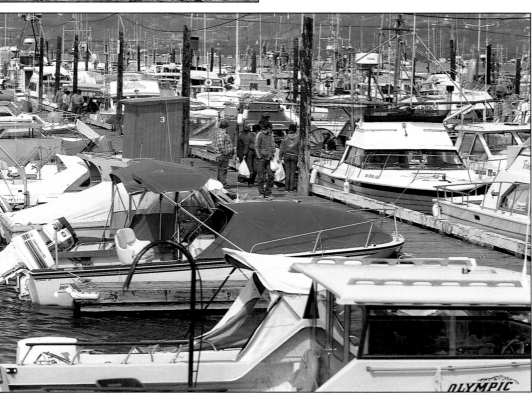

Homer marina.

A Russian Orthodox ceremony on St. George Island.

Facing page: an Orthodox priest, Unalaska.

Below: St. Nicholas Russian Orthodox Church, Juneau.

The Church of St. Nicholas at Eklutna, near Anchorage.

Right: a Russian chapel at Eklutna.

A Christian cemetery in Kotzebue.

"Spirit houses" mark Indian graves at Eklutna.

The Russian Orthodox church at Ninilchik on the Kenai Peninsula.

Below: a wayside church at Anvik on the Yukon River.

*Colorful wooden
houses protect Indian
dead near Anchorage.*

*Fond remembrance –
artificial flowers
withstand the cold.*

*Color plays a large part
in the design of an
Indian grave.*

Sunset over Iditarod, a ghost town in western Alaska.

Fairbanks countryside.

*Black and ice blue –
Iditarod ruins.*

*Winter along the
Sterling Highway.*

*Portage Glacier, a
great tourist attraction.*

*The Alaska Range,
girdled with glaciers.*

*A winter sunset over
Unalakleet.*

*Facing page: moonrise
over the Alaska Range.*

The Chena River, Fairbanks.

Below: central Fairbanks, the heart of the Interior.

An aerial view of Anchorage, Alaska's biggest city.

Below: Seward on the Kenai Peninsula.

*Cook Monument,
Anchorage.*

*A cold day in
Anchorage.*

*Fourth Avenue,
Anchorage.*

Knik Arm – ice cold in Anchorage.

Nome's bleak midwinter setting.

Central Anchorage skyscrapers.

Letting sleeping dogs lie – regardless of the weather.

Facing page: a hardy husky bitch and pup.

Below left: an Alaskan husky, born to the snow.

Huskys are distru of strangers and good watchdogs.

Dreaming of a warm bed.

Did somebody say "mush?"

Hardworking huskies are worth their weight in gold.

Teamed-up and waiting for the off.

Above: at rest in the shade.

Old friends take time out along the trail.

A frosty brow – the husky's coat is very dense.

The best sled dogs are always eager to run.

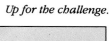

Up for the challenge.

The warmest spot.

Facing page: finding shelter wherever possible.

Left: a trawler at work in Glacier Bay.

Facing page: the catch of the day in Homer.

Below: fishing from the shore, Turnagain Arm.

The one that didn't get away.

Left: fisheries earn $1.3 billion a year for Alaska.

Fishing weirs.

Fish-drying racks.

Below: an Inuit boy and his fish dryer.

Unloading a shrimp boat in Petersburg.

Fresh fish for dinner tonight.

Right: a Bering Sea satellite station, Nome.

Natural gas storage tanks – just some of Alaska's mineral wealth.

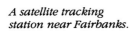

A satellite tracking station near Fairbanks.

Left: a bush pilot's landmark.

Farming the old-fashioned way.

Right: a gold dredger near Fairbanks.

Right: panning for gold in the environs of Fairbanks.

An abandoned gold dredger.

*Highway One, south of
Anchorage.*

*Campbell Lake,
Anchorage.*

*A retreat along the
Seward Highway.*

A sleepy guard dog, Kotzebue.

Driftwood and a husky puppy, Nome.

*Everything in its place
– a Nome shack.*

*Right: driftwood for
winter's fires.*

*Nome residents pose for
the camera.*

Right: Libby Riddles and her Inuit friends.

Walker Glacier near the Alsek River.

Rafting on the Mendenall River.

A backyard cookout with fresh-caught fish.

Facing page: Eagle's Nest ski resort, Juneau.

Marshmallow toasting at Juneau.

Left: a salmon bake at the mining museum, Juneau.

Facing page: a spick-and-span beach house, Homer.

*A river flows fast in the
thaw near Valdez.*

*The Susitna River,
Denali National Park.*

*Left: the snaking
Yukon River.*

*Below: the Mendenhall
Glacier's icy tongue.*

*Below: a winter
mountain sentinal.*

*White water, Denali
National Park.*

Winter trees mirrored in a peaceful pool.

Drowned trees in moose country.

Spring thaw in Denali National Park.

Below: a quiet corner along the Richardson Highway.

Denali National Park – protected forever.

Below: spring sun highlights the Alaska Range.

The Muir Inlet Glacier meets its end.

Frozen wastes across the river near Nome.

Ice floes like frozen fish fillets at Nome.

Norton Sound, ice-bound and windswept.

Miniature mountain peaks – ice floes in Turnagain Arm.

*Almost there – the end
of the Iditarod Trail.*